END TIMES PROPHECIES

Discover what the future holds for you.

Written by Paul Kocourek

Contents

INTRODUCTION

Since the beginning of time, people have wondered what the future holds, particularly what would happen near the end of time. Over the history of Man, there have been many attempts to tell the future. In the present time, there has been more than ever a deep desire to know the future.

There have been predictions by both psychics and charlatans, but they are unreliable and all fall far short of reality. To know what the future holds, we have to have a source that is reliable and unimpeachable. That source needs to have a perfect record of fulfilled prophecies, as evidenced by history, never missing a single time. Such a source we do not find in Man, but in the God who made Man.

Bible prophecy or biblical prophecy comprises the passages of the Bible that reflect communications from God to humans through prophets.[1]

The record for fulfilled Bible prophecies is 100%. History gives us a picture of past prophecies that have been fulfilled. But more to the purpose of this book, the perfection of their fulfillments gives us confidence that prophecies that are yet in our future are absolutely going to happen. To be fair, I do not intend this book to be exhaustive.

Prophecies started in the Bible in the OT (Old Testament) book of Genesis, the book of beginnings, and prophecies for the future – OUR future – are found in the NT (New Testament), particularly in the four gospels and the book of Revelation. The scary word apocalypse draws to mind many Hollywood disaster movies, which have been used to make financial fortunes through scaring the pants off people. Most movie goers take a sigh of relief when the movie is over, glad that the nightmarish scenes aren't real. Or, are they? The word apocalypse comes from the Greek word for the book of Revelation, "ἀποκάλυψις *apokalypsis.*" It literally means, to take the cover off, or reveal. Hence ἀποκάλυψις *apokalypsis* means Revelation, or the revealing of the future, because it takes the cover off what lays ahead in the future, our future.

This book will look at various ancient fulfilled prophecies which to show the reliability of Bible prophecies, and then in a later chapter, look as the cover is being lifted off to reveal what is absolutely going to happen in the future. Warning! The prophetic picture of the future is not pretty. But there is hope.

Babylon Will Rule Over Judah for 70 Years

You can read the first such prophecies in Jeremiah 25:11-12. This prophecy was written sometime from 626 to about 586 BC and was not fulfilled until about 609 BC to 539 BC (approximately 50 years later, depending on your calculation)

> "...This whole country will become a desolate wasteland, and these nations will serve the king of Babylon seventy years. But when the seventy years are fulfilled, I will punish the king of Babylon and his nation, the land of the Babylonians, for their guilt," declares the Lord, "and will make it desolate forever" (Jeremiah 25:11-12).

In this passage of Scripture, Jeremiah said that the Jews would suffer 70 years of Babylonian domination, and that after this was over, Babylon would be punished. Both parts of this prophecy were fulfilled! In 609 BC, Babylon captured the last Assyrian king and took over the holdings of the Assyrian empire, which included the land of Israel. Babylon then began to flex its muscles by taking many Jews as captives to Babylon and by destroying Jerusalem and the Temple. This domination of the Jews ended in 539 BC, when Cyrus, a leader of Persians and Medes, conquered Babylon, bringing an end to the empire. The prophecy also had another fulfillment: the Babylonians destroyed Jerusalem's Temple in 586 BC, but the Jews rebuilt it and consecrated it 70 years later, in 516 BC. Restoring the Temple showed, in a very important way, that the effects of Babylonian domination had indeed come to an end.[2]

The Prophecies of Babylon, Nineveh, Tyre and Edom

Let's take a look at a few Bible prophecies that were fulfilled about 2500 years ago when the ancient kingdoms and cities of Babylon, Nineveh, Tyre and Edom were destroyed. The Bible makes the assertion that these entities were destroyed because they had sought to destroy the Holy Land of Israel and the people of Israel (the Jews).[3]

Babylon's Gates Will Open for Cyrus

A remarkable prophecy had been made about a future ruler, Cyrus. What is so amazing is that the prophecy had been made naming the future ruler as Cyrus, before Cyrus had even been born!

If you read Isaiah 45:1 (written perhaps between 701 and 681 BC), you will find a prophecy that was ultimately fulfilled hundreds of years later in 539 BC.

"This is what the Lord says to his anointed, to Cyrus, whose right hand I take hold of to subdue nations before him and to strip kings of their armor, to open doors before him so that gates will not be shut..." (Isaiah 45:1).

In this passage, the prophet said God would open the gates of Babylon for Cyrus and his attacking army. Despite Babylon's remarkable defenses, which included moats, and walls that were more than 70-feet thick and 300-feet high (with 250 watchtowers) Cyrus was able to enter the city and conquer it. Cyrus and his troops accomplished it by diverting the flow of the Euphrates River into a large lake basin. Cyrus then was able to march his army across the riverbed and into the city.[4]

Babylon's Kingdom Will Be Permanently Overthrown

In Isaiah 13:19 (written between 701 and 681 BC) there exists yet another prophecy that was not fulfilled until 539 BC.

"Babylon, the jewel of kingdoms, the glory of the Babylonians' pride, will be overthrown by God like Sodom and Gomorrah" (Isaiah 13:19).

Here, Isaiah tells us that Babylon would be overthrown, permanently. History confirms the fact that following Cyrus' destruction of Babylon in 539 BC, it never again rose to power as an empire. You've got to remember, however, that before the time of Cyrus, Babylon had been defeated by the Assyrian Empire as well, But Babylon was able to recover and later conquer the Assyrian Empire. In light of this reality, I'm sure many people doubted Isaiah when he proclaimed this prophecy. In spite of this, and just as Isaiah predicted, the Babylonian empire was defeated, and never recovered from Cyrus' conquest.[5]

The Jews Will Survive Babylonian Rule and Return Home

In Jeremiah 32:36-37, (written from about 626 and 586 BC), yet another prophet makes a bold prediction that was ultimately fulfilled in 536 BC.

"You are saying about this city, 'By the sword, famine and plague it will be handed over to the king of Babylon'; but this is what the Lord, the God of Israel, says: I will surely gather them from all the lands where I banish them in my furious anger and great wrath; I will bring them back to this place and let them live in safety" (Jeremiah 32:36-37).

In this passage, Jeremiah said that the Jews would survive their captivity in Babylon and return home, and both parts of this prophecy were ultimately fulfilled. Many Jews had been taken as captives to Babylon beginning around 605 BC. But, in 538 BC, they were released from captivity and many eventually returned to their homeland. [6]

Again and again, the prophets of Israel gave the message, "Thus says the Lord God…", making the claim that what was given by those prophets were the very words of God Himself.

Chapter Two: OT Prophecies fulfilled in the NT

Bethlehem would see the birth of Jesus Christ

Around the world, people celebrate Christmas time. Many people sing carols, and radio stations play, a famous and beloved carol, O Little Town of Bethlehem. What many do not know is that the birth of Jesus Christ in Bethlehem was prophesied in an OT prophecy.

2 But thou, Bethlehem Ephratah, though thou be little among the thousands of Judah, yet out of thee shall he come forth unto me that is to be ruler in Israel; whose goings forth have been from of old, from everlasting. (Micah 5:2)

The story is well known how because of a Roman census, Joseph and pregnant Mary had to leave for the town of his ancestor, David, Bethlehem. Mary gave birth to Jesus in a stable in that town.

The land of Israel would be reborn

A prophecy that got the ball rolling, so to speak for modern days fulfillments, is **Isaiah 66:8**, prophesying that the nation of Israel would be born in one day.

8 Who hath heard such a thing? who hath seen such things? Shall the earth be made to bring forth in one day? or shall a nation be born at once? for as soon as Zion travailed, she brought forth her children.

That prophecy was made about 700 years before Christ.

The Romans had conquered and evicted the Jews and renamed their land after the ancient enemies of Israel, the Philistines and so the land was renamed by the Romans as Palestine. For century after century, the Jews had no land they could call home, and were for so many years labeled the "wandering Jews." Yet Prophecy declared that Israel would be reborn, and so it was 2600 years later on May 14, 1948.

The Jews would return to their homeland

Ezekiel 37:11-12, 21

11 Then he said unto me, Son of man, these bones are the whole house of Israel: behold, they say, Our bones are dried, and our hope is lost: we are cut off for our parts. 12 Therefore prophesy and say unto them, Thus saith the Lord God; Behold, O my people, I will open your graves, and cause you to come up out of your graves, and bring you into the land of Israel.

21 And say unto them, Thus saith the Lord GOD; Behold, I will take the children of Israel from among the heathen, whither they be gone, and will gather them on every side, and bring them into their own land: [7]

Israel would export produce to the world

Isaiah 27:6

6 He shall cause them that come of Jacob to take root: Israel shall blossom and bud, and fill the face of the world with fruit.

Israel has become one of the largest exporters of produce to the world.[8] I have eaten chocolate candies with an orange jelly filling made from oranges from Israel (they were delicious!)

Israel would plant forests and trees

Isaiah 41:18-20

[18] I will open rivers in high places, and fountains in the midst of the valleys: I will make the wilderness a pool of water, and the dry land springs of water. [19] I will plant in the wilderness the cedar, the shittah tree, and the myrtle, and the oil tree; I will set in the desert the fir tree, and the pine, and the box tree together: [20] That they may see, and know, and consider, and understand together, that the hand of the LORD hath done this, and the Holy One of Israel hath created it. [9]

Israel would recapture Jerusalem
Zechariah 12:6

[6] In that day will I make the governors of Judah like an hearth of fire among the wood, and like a torch of fire in a sheaf; and they shall devour all the people round about, on the right hand and on the left: and Jerusalem shall be inhabited again in her own place, even in Jerusalem.

This recapture happened in June of 1967 in what is called The Six Day War. [10]

Temple to be destroyed, not one stone left upon another

[1] And Jesus went out, and departed from the temple: and his disciples came to him for to shew him the buildings of the temple. [2] And Jesus said unto them, See ye not all these things? verily I say unto you, There shall not be left here one stone upon another, that shall not be thrown down. (Matthew 24:1-2)

Later in 70 D, the Roman General Titus and the Roman legions fulfilled this exactly as prophesied.

As the fire set by the Romans in 70 AD raged through the sanctuary in the Temple, quantities of silver and gold, which had been placed there for safe-keeping, melted and ran down between the stones. Roman soldiers tore apart the stones to retrieve the gold and silver, literally leaving "not one stone left upon another"[12]

Jesus prophesied that He would be betrayed

The Apostles of Jesus were in a unique position: They were able to see with their own eyes whether Jesus was the fulfillment of various Old Testament prophecies about the Messiah. And, they were able to see whether the prophecies that Jesus gave in regards to himself and his followers were being fulfilled.

Jesus prophesied, for example, that one of the 12 Apostles would betray him:

20 When evening came, Jesus was reclining at the table with the Twelve. 21 And while they were eating, he said, "Truly I tell you, one of you will betray me." (Matthew 26:20,21, NIV)

A short time later, Judas Iscariot betrayed Jesus. The betrayal was followed by the arrest, trial, and execution of Jesus. [13]

Jesus prophesied that the Apostles would desert him

In Matthew 26:31,32, Jesus alluded to an Old Testament passage found in Zechariah 13:7 and prophesied that his Apostles soon would flee from him:

Then Jesus told them, "This very night you will all fall away on account of me, for it is written:

" 'I will strike the shepherd, and the sheep of the flock will be scattered.'

But after I have risen, I will go ahead of you into Galilee." (Matthew 26:31,32, NIV)

Later, Judas Iscariot, who betrayed Jesus, led a crowd of armed people to the place where Jesus and some of his followers were staying. Jesus was arrested and the Apostles fled:

Then all the disciples deserted him and fled. (Matthew 26:56b, NIV) [14]

Jesus prophesied that Peter would disown him

After Jesus informed the Apostles, in Matthew 26, that they soon would abandon him, Peter responded that he would never abandon Jesus, even if everyone else did.

Jesus then specifically addressed Peter, prophesying that Peter would deny knowing Jesus:

"I tell you the truth," Jesus answered, "this very night, before the rooster crows, you will disown me three times." (Matthew 26:34, NIV)

Soon after, Jesus was arrested and the Apostles scattered away from him. Later that night, as described in Matthew 26:69-75, Peter was approached by people who recognized him as an associate of Jesus. Peter denied what they said, claiming that he didn't know Jesus.

After Peter's denial, a rooster crowed, prompting Peter to remember the words that Jesus had spoken:

Then he began to call down curses on himself and he swore to them, "I don't know the man!" Immediately a rooster crowed. Then Peter remembered the word Jesus had spoken: "Before the rooster crows, you will disown me three times." And he went outside and wept bitterly. (Matthew 26:74,75, NIV) [15]

Jesus prophesied that the Jews would be exiled

In Luke 21:24, Jesus prophesied that the Jews would be exiled from their land. This prophecy was fulfilled, beginning about 40 years later.

The Jews fought two wars against the Romans in the hopes of reclaiming independence for their homeland. The first war ended in 70 AD and the second war ended in 135 AD. In both wars, the Jews were defeated and forced into exile.

Josephus, the Jewish historian who witnessed the fall of Jerusalem during the first century, claimed that nearly 100,000 people were forced into exile:

"Now the number of those that were carried captive during this whole war was collected to be ninety-seven thousand;"
- Josephus, *The Wars of the Jews,* Book VI, Chapter 9.

The conquest during the second century culminated with another exile, as well as a decree prohibiting the exiled Jews from returning to Jerusalem:

"When the siege had lasted a long time, and the rebels had been driven to the last extremity by hunger and thirst, and the instigator of the rebellion had suffered his just punishment, the whole nation was prohibited from this time on by a decree, and by the commands of Adrian, from ever going up to the country about Jerusalem. For the emperor gave orders that they should not even see from a distance the land of their fathers. Such is the account of Aristo of Pella. And thus, when the city had been emptied of the Jewish nation and had suffered the total destruction of its ancient inhabitants, it was colonized by a different race, and the Roman city which subsequently arose changed its name and was called AElia, in honor of the emperor AElius Adrian."
- *The Church History of Eusebius,* Book IV, Chapter 6.

The extent to which the decree was enforced is unclear. Some Jews later returned from exile. Today, according to some estimates involving the world's Jewish population, about one-third are residing within the modern state of Israel and about two-thirds are residing in communities all over the world.

Here is that prophecy in Luke 21:24:

They will fall by the sword and will be taken as prisoners to all the nations. Jerusalem will be trampled on by the Gentiles until the times of the Gentiles are fulfilled. (Luke 21:24, NIV) [16]

Chapter Four: Prophecies yet to come fulfilled in our future

Warning! As said in the introduction, the prophetic picture of the future is not pretty. Now comes the scary part, in that it will come upon everyone on the Earth.

Yet, there is hope to escape all this, which we will cover later.

We will start with Daniel's 70 Weeks prophecy.

To understand the future, we need to first go back to the past. Long ago, God called Abram (later renamed Abraham), and promised to make his descendants more numerous than he could count.

"And He took him outside and said, 'Now look toward the heavens, and count the stars, if you are able to count them.' And He said to him, 'So shall your descendants be.' Then he believed in the LORD, and He reckoned it to him as righteousness." (Genesis 15:5–6)

God also told him his descendants would serve as slaves:

"God said to Abram, 'Know for certain that your descendants will be strangers in a land that is not theirs, where they will be enslaved and oppressed four hundred years. But I will also judge the nation whom they will serve, and afterward they will come out with many possessions.'" (Genesis 15:13–14)

This latter prophecy was fulfilled, and the book of Exodus tells the story. Israel went through a time of getting settled in, which is covered in the book of Judges. Then God sent prophets and gave kings to the people of Israel. As the centuries passed, the people of Israel kept falling into idolatry and other disobedience to God. Someone has said it is as though Israel had made a national pastime of disobeying God. Finally, God had had enough, and sent Nebuchadnezzar of Babylon to overthrow Israel. Through the prophet Jeremiah, God told them:

"For thus says the LORD, 'When seventy years have been completed for Babylon, I will visit you and fulfill My good word to you, to bring you back to this place.'" (Jeremiah 29:10)

Shift forward to the book of Daniel. Daniel had been a young man, a teenager, when he and three Hebrew friends were taken into captivity in Babylon by Nebuchadnezzar. After some adventures, Daniel grew old, and was reading his Scriptures when he came across the prophecy in Jeremiah.

"In the first year of his reign, I, Daniel, observed in the books the number of the years which was revealed as the word of the LORD to Jeremiah the prophet for the completion of the desolations of Jerusalem, namely, seventy years." (Daniel 9:2)

Daniel had been there almost 70 years and the time of Jerusalem's desolations was almost over. He set himself to pray and fast and seek God about the matter. God sent the angel Gabriel, the same angel who announced the Virgin Birth to a young Jewish woman named Mary, to tell Daniel that Israel's destiny would be completed, not in 70 years, but in 70 "weeks" of years, or 70 x 7 years = 490 years. These years are comprised of lunar months of 30 days each, so each of these prophesied years is 360 days, not 365 days as seen in our western calendars.

"Seventy weeks have been decreed for your people and your holy city, to finish the transgression, to make an end of sin, to make atonement for iniquity, to bring in everlasting righteousness, to seal up vision and prophecy and to anoint the most holy place." (Daniel 9:24)

The starting point in time for the 490 years was clearly identified by Gabriel:

"So you are to know and discern that from the issuing of a decree to restore and rebuild Jerusalem unto Messiah the Prince there will be seven weeks and sixty-two weeks; it will be built again, with plaza and moat, even in times of distress." (Daniel 9:25)

Jerusalem had been destroyed by Nebuchadnezzar and lay in desolate ruins. Years later, Nehemiah, a Jew who was a cupbearer to the king, obtained the prophesied decree to restore and rebuild Jerusalem:

"And I said to the king, 'If it please the king, let letters be given me for the governors of the provinces beyond the river, that they may allow me to pass through until I come to Judah, and a letter to Asaph the keeper of the king's forest, that he may give me timber to make beams for the gates of the fortress which is by the temple, for the wall of the city and for the house to which I will go.' And the king granted them to me because the good hand of my God was on me." (Nehemiah 2:7–8)

That event in Nehemiah's day gave the starting time of the 490 years.

Now, while 70 weeks (490 years) is the total time span for the prophecy, the time the Messiah would come would occur after 69 weeks had elapsed (i.e., the "seven weeks and sixty-two weeks" in verse 25, where 7 + 62 = 69). As the 69-week period (483 years) came to its conclusion, on the very last day, Jesus was presented to Israel as the Messiah on Palm Sunday. At

Jesus' command, His disciples obtained a donkey colt to ride on in fulfillment of prophecy.

"This took place to fulfill what was spoken through the prophet: 'Say to the daughter of Zion, "Behold your King is coming to you, gentle, and mounted on a donkey, even on a colt, the foal of a beast of burden."' The disciples went and did just as Jesus had instructed them, and brought the donkey and colt, and laid their coats on them; and He sat on the coats. Most of the crowd spread their coats in the road, and others were cutting branches from the trees and spreading them in the road. The crowds going ahead of Him, and those who followed, were shouting, 'Hosanna to the Son of David; Blessed is He who comes in the name of the Lord; Hosanna in the highest!'" (Matthew 21:4–9)

Though the people greeted Him with Messianic fervor, He knew they did not truly believe in Him and would turn on Him to crucify Him only days later.

"When He approached Jerusalem, He saw the city and wept over it, saying, 'If you had known in this day, even you, the things which make for peace! But now they have been hidden from your eyes...because you did not recognize the time of your visitation.'" (Luke 19:41–42, 44b)

What did Jesus mean by "the time of your visitation?" If the Jewish rulers had believed their Scriptures, they would have calculated those 69 weeks of Daniel's prophecy to find out when Messiah would be presented to them. Their own book of Nehemiah gave them the starting date, and they could have checked their calendar calculations to realize the last day of the 69th week was upon them—here was Jesus riding in to Messianic acclaim in fulfillment of the prophecy in Zechariah

9:9! But they didn't believe it. They "did not recognize the time of [their] visitation."

The prophecy concerning the 70 weeks continues:

"Then after the sixty-two weeks the Messiah will be cut off and have nothing, and the people of the prince who is to come will destroy the city and the sanctuary. And its end will come with a flood; even to the end there will be war; desolations are determined." (Daniel 9:26)

The 7 weeks (49 years) had elapsed, followed by 62 more weeks (additional 434 years). The prophecy says "after" the 62 weeks, the Messiah "will be cut off," which is another way of saying Messiah would be put to death. We know that Jesus made His appearance as Messiah on Palm Sunday, which was the last day of the 483 years, and just a few days later He was put on trial, crucified, died and was buried. The following Sunday He rose from the dead.

This sequence reveals several important things. First, God's prophecies ALWAYS come true. Since prophecies in the past became 100 percent true, so other prophecies in the future can be trusted to be fulfilled. Second, the first 69 weeks were all sequential—as soon as one week was finished, the next began. Third, the final week of the prophecy, the 70th week, is NOT sequential. In other words, it didn't follow immediately after the end of the 69th week, but actually still awaits a future fulfillment.

There are several developments in the 70 weeks prophecy that support a gap in time between the 69th and 70th weeks. First, the Messiah being cut off happened several days after the 69th week, but before the 70th week. Second, a prophecy was made that

Jerusalem and the temple would both be destroyed, which Titus and the Roman legions fulfilled when they overthrew Jerusalem and destroyed the temple in A.D. 70. Another part in the Daniel prophecy further demonstrating a gap between the 69th and 70th weeks is found in Daniel 9:26b: "And its end will come with a flood; even to the end there will be war; desolations are determined."

A long period of time would have to occur between the 69th and 70th weeks if war would be ongoing "even to the end." Moreover, the land would be in desolation for a long, indefinite period "even to the end." Yet, because the first 69 weeks happened exactly as prophesied, including the rebuilding of Jerusalem and the temple, followed hundreds of years later by the redestruction of Jerusalem and the temple, then we know that the 70th week is still certain to come to a prophetic fulfillment.

After Messiah was "cut off," God put His plans for Israel on hold and chose to work in and through the Church. The long period of desolation for Israel between the 69th and 70th weeks is filled with the Church Age. However, once the Church is Raptured, God will resume dealing with Israel to fulfill her destiny, and the great cosmic countdown of the 70th week will begin! It is by this 70th week that we know the Tribulation period will be 7 years long, where each year is 360 days.

In the New Testament, the Apostle Paul wrote of Israel and the Gentiles in word imagery, contrasting a cultivated olive tree (Israel) and a wild olive tree (Gentiles). He made the point that God broke off Israel like olive branches broken off the cultivated tree, and grafted in the wild Gentiles. (Romans 11:17–20) A day is coming when the wild olive branches of the Gentiles will themselves be broken off, and the cultivated olive branches of the Jews will be grafted in again. (Romans 11:21–24)

Finally, Paul put it all together:

"For I do not want you, brethren, to be uninformed of this mystery—so that you will not be wise in your own estimation— that a partial hardening has happened to Israel until the fullness of the Gentiles has come in." (Romans 11:25)

The "fullness of the Gentiles" is the time in the Church Age when as many Gentiles as will be saved is completed. When that fullness is reached, the Rapture takes the Church out of the way; the Gentile "branches" are broken off, and the Jewish "branches" are regrafted in. This is why Revelation turns Jewish in style and flavor in chapter 4 and beyond—the Rapture ends the time of the Gentiles, and the time of Israel returns.

Remember, too, God's declaration through Gabriel is that the prophecy had been decreed "for your people and your holy city". The final seven years of Daniel's 70th Week (what we call the Tribulation period) is all about the physical descendants of Israel and the physical city of Jerusalem, not the Church consisting of saved individuals from every nation, tribe, people and tongue. Those final seven years are Jewish in God's plans, focus and intent. He is finishing up promises made to His people Israel. God always keeps His promises..

Since the 70th week (consisting of 7 lunar years, each having 360 days) is the framework for the coming Tribulation period, there are other things we can learn about the Tribulation period from this prophecy:

"And he will make a firm covenant with the many for one week, but in the middle of the week he will put a stop to sacrifice and grain offering; and on the wing of abominations will come one who makes desolate, even until a complete destruction, one that is decreed, is poured out on the one who makes desolate." (Daniel 9:27)

First, we can see that a covenant of 7 years' duration will be put into effect. Since the 70 weeks prophecy is about Israel's destiny, Israel would certainly be involved in it. But, notice something history reveals: After the Romans overthrew the nation of Israel, there was NO nation of Israel for some 1,900 years! So, for there to be a covenant involving Israel, the Jews would have to return to their land again and become a nation once more. To the astonishment of people around the world, this happened on May 14, 1948.

Second, covenants are by their nature not just with one person or party. This covenant is "with the many." Likely it will involve other nations as well as Israel.

Third, we see the covenant lasts only for one-half of the agreed time, for the one who makes the covenant breaks it at the middle point. The "prince who is to come" (verse 26) is the "he" (verse 27) who makes the "firm covenant" and then breaks it halfway through. The people who destroyed Jerusalem (verse 26) were the Romans, so the covenant maker and breaker (verse 27) is a ruler over a modern empire arising out of the old Roman Empire. Bible scholars call this man the Antichrist.

Fourth, notice that the old Jewish sacrificial system will be once more practiced in Israel, for the Antichrist puts "a stop to sacrifice and grain offering."

Fifth, since sacrifices and grain offerings will once again be practiced in Israel, and they were practiced in a temple of God, this means a temple will be built again in Jerusalem.

Sixth, it tells us that in the middle of the seven covenanted years, the Antichrist commits a hateful act, an "abomination," that makes the temple desolate, meaning it will be unfit for the purposes of calling on the true God. This "abomination of desolation" is pivotal to all that happens in the Tribulation period's seven years.

Seventh, this prophecy tells us that the desolation caused by the Antichrist will continue until he is completely destroyed.

It has been said that there will be no material advantage to being alive on earth during the time of the reign of the Antichrist. This is so true. The seven years of the Tribulation period will be so severe that Jesus said, "Unless those days had been cut short, no life would have been saved." (Matthew 24:22a)

The God of the universe calls us to repent, to change our minds and very hearts now, while there is still yet time:

"For He says, 'At the acceptable time I listened to you and on the day of salvation I helped you.' Behold, now is 'the acceptable time,' behold, now is 'the day of salvation.'" (2 Corinthians 6:2)

There is a popular saying, that there is good news and there is bad news, and the question is often asked, which one do you want to hear first?

We will answer that: first the bad news.
Sit tight for a truly apocalyptic future.

In Ezekiel 38, there is a prophesied allied invasion from the north of Israel. Students of Bible prophecy called it by the names identified in the chapter, Gog and Magog. This is modern day

Russia. Its first listed ally is Persia, known today as Iran. Another ally is identified by the names Gomer: the Cimmerians; and the house of Togarmah 11, which is modern day Turkey. Other allies given are Ethiopia and Libya. Russia, Iran and Turkey have recently announced to the world their solidarity with each other. All three are present in the nation of Syria to the north of Israel, and it is from that north the prophesied invasion is to come. (Ezekiel 39:2)

The army might of the invading forces of the combined armies of Russia, Turkey and Iran, seems irresistible, but the prophecy also says God will take a direct hand and crush those invading armies on the mountain of Israel, (i.e. the Golan Heights), leaving alive only the sixth part of those invading hordes. (Ezekiel 39:3-4)

There is some trepidation where the prophecy (Ezekiel 39:6) says the Lord promises to send "fire" on Magog (the land of Russia) and on those who "dwell carelessly in the isles (i.e. coastlands)", possibly an allusion to God judging Russia and its long-time enemy the United States, with that "fire" representing fire from Him, like that poured out on Sodom and Gomorrah, falling on both sides.

As said previously, back in the OT book of Daniel, a prophecy was given, called the Seventy Weeks prophecy, which covered 70 weeks of years (where each week = 7 years). The first 69 weeks were fulfilled, ending on Palm Sunday when Jesus rode into the streets of Jerusalem on the back of a donkey in fulfillment of a prophecy.

Rejoice greatly, O daughter of Zion; shout, O daughter of Jerusalem: behold, thy King cometh unto thee: he is just, and having salvation; lowly, and riding upon an ass, and upon a colt the foal of an ass. (Zechariah 9:9)

That last of Daniel's prophecy, 70th week, however, has not yet been fulfilled, but is for a future fulfillment. People commonly call these last seven years, The Tribulation.

Jesus gave a prophecy about the future of the people of Israel, and His prophecies were repeated in the book of Revelation. We can compare Jesus' words in Matthew 24 with his words in Revelation 6, for they are parallel to each other..

Here is a rundown of what is to come.
Let us look at some rather unnerving math about the 70th Week (aka the Tribulation).

The Bible teaches in Revelation chapter 6 that, by the time the first four Seals have been unsealed, 1/4th of the Earth will be slain. That is one-fourth of everybody on Earth! Given present global populations, that death toll amounts to about two billion (not million) people, meaning an incredible loss of life!

8 And I looked, and behold a pale horse: and his name that sat on him was Death, and Hell followed with him. And power was given unto them over the fourth part of the earth, to kill with sword, and with hunger, and with death, and with the beasts of the earth. (Revelation 6:8)

Now, the elements of what that prophecy says are as follows: "To kill with the sword" is the 2nd Seal, the rider on the red horse:

3 And when he had opened the second seal, I heard the second beast say, Come and see.4 And there went out another horse that was red: and power was given to him that sat thereon to take

peace from the earth, and that they should kill one another: and there was given unto him a great sword. (Revelation 6:3-4)

The rider on the red horse wields a "mega" (Greek μέγας megas) or "great" sword. To a world that has seen World War I and then World War II, this means World War III. Given the nuclear arsenals on a hair trigger in the nations of the world, this means a war where all bets are off and nukes get used.

"and with hunger" is the 3rd Seal, the rider on a black horse, an incredible worldwide killing famine causing mass starvation. As I write this, food shortages are already happening globally: Once WWIII breaks out, it is likely there will be limited or no grain shipments around the world to feed the global population, especially for fear of radioactivity if nukes are used.

5 And when he had opened the third seal, I heard the third beast say, Come and see. And I beheld, and lo a black horse; and he that sat on him had a pair of balances in his hand. 6 And I heard a voice in the midst of the four beasts say, A measure of wheat for a penny, and three measures of barley for a penny; and see thou hurt not the oil and the wine. (Revelation 6:5-6)

That "penny" is, back in that day, a denarius, commonly a day's wage. For a loaf of bread to cost a denarius, is saying that it will take all a man can earn in a day to buy just one load of bread. The grain barley, being not so much in demand, could sell for three loaves for a denarius. Famine strikes the earth! Concerning the statement about "hurt not the oil and the wine", oil is not the petroleum we all know about in the news about the number of barrels of oil sold and bought, but was olive oil used for lamps for light in the house, for cooking, and for medicinal use. Oil and wine are both products of the Middle East and Mediterranean regions, so it is likely that WWIII will not affect those regions of the world.

That fourth Seal also says, "and with death". For what form(s) that death will take, we need only to look at a parallel passage in Matthew 24: "and pestilences, and earthquakes, in divers places." (Matthew 24:7b). So, the death toll from the 4th Seal will include people dying from highly contagious pandemic plagues/pestilences, and from devastating earthquakes, landslides and volcanic eruptions.

"and with the beasts of the earth" is the result of the catastrophic global famine, such that animals are starving so badly that they attack and eat people.

Moreover, that is not all the bad news, for there is more, even worse! Jesus gave a prophecy about the Tribulation's woes.

25 And there shall be signs in the sun, and in the moon, and in the stars; and upon the earth distress of nations, with perplexity; the sea and the waves roaring; 26 Men's hearts failing them for fear, and for looking after those things which are coming on the earth: for the powers of heaven shall be shaken. (Luke 21:25-26)

This prophecy calls for distress of nations with perplexity, which means, distressed people being confused and at a loss of what to do. Of particular note is the phrase "the sea and the waves roaring." This foretells killer hurricanes making the seas and waves roaring. Moreover, it may also include tsunamis because of earthquakes and volcanic eruptions. The time of the Tribulation will likely also include wild weather on land, with killer thunderstorms, tornados and hail storms.

The things going on around the world will be SO bad, that Jesus said, "Men's hearts failing them for fear, and for looking after those things which are coming on the earth: for the powers of heaven shall be shaken." The Greek for men's heart "failing" them is ἀποψύχω *apopsychō,* which literally means "to breathe out life, expire." In effect, the prophecy is saying that things will be so fearful, that people will die of heart attacks, literally frightened to death!

Don't be one of them! Take the escape clause covered in the next chapter!

By the way, these prophesied things are for just the first half (first 1260 days) of the 70th Week (aka the Tribulation). It gets even worse for the inhabitants of the world in the second half. You might wonder, what could be worse than WWIII, mass starvation, and widespread fatal diseases? Prophecy gives us the answer. The cause behind the hand of God not being lifted again Mankind for merely political or other physical reasons, but because of moral reasons. These things are happening because Mankind has shaken its rebellious fist in the face of its Creator, and in the face of the Savior who came to Earth to save us from ourselves.

So much more will be going on during the Tribulation. There will be a worldwide empire ruling over all the Earth, the empire of the Antichrist. It has been said that he will be the most evil man who has ever lived, like the devil incarnate. He will have a sheerly evil purpose supported by Satan directly (who is called in Revelation 13, "the dragon"). The Apostle Paul labeled the Antichrist as "the man of sin" and "the son of perdition."

[3] Let no man deceive you by any means: for that day shall not come, except there come a falling away first, and that man of sin be revealed, the son of perdition; (2 Thessalonians 2:3)

In Revelation, he is called "the beast" and he demands to be worshiped!

[4] And they worshipped the dragon [Satan] which gave power unto the beast [the Antichrist]: and they worshipped the beast,

saying, Who is like unto the beast? who is able to make war with him? ⁵ And there was given unto him a mouth speaking great things and blasphemies; and power was given unto him to continue forty and two months. ⁶ And he opened his mouth in blasphemy against God, to blaspheme his name, and his tabernacle, and them that dwell in heaven. ⁷ And it was given unto him to make war with the saints, and to overcome them: and power was given him over all kindreds, and tongues, and nations. ⁸ And all that dwell upon the earth shall worship him, whose names are not written in the book of life of the Lamb slain from the foundation of the world. *Revelation 13:4-8)

It is also prophesied that if anyone will not worship him or take his 666 Mark, that person will be slain.

¹⁵ And he had power to give life unto the image of the beast, that the image of the beast should both speak, and cause that as many as would not worship the image of the beast should be killed. And he causeth all, both small and great, rich and poor, free and bond, to receive a mark in their right hand, or in their foreheads: (Revelation 13:15-16)

If you are thinking this is the stuff of nightmares, you are right, but unlike a nightmare from which a person can safely awaken, this is real.

Someone might think, well, I will avoid getting killed, so I'll will just take that 666 Mark.

But that is fatally foolish, for another prophecy speaks to that very thing.

⁹ And the third angel followed them, saying with a loud voice, If any man worship the beast and his image, and receive his mark in his forehead, or in his hand, ¹⁰ The same shall drink of the wine of the wrath of God, which is poured out without mixture into the cup of his indignation; and he shall be tormented with fire and brimstone in the presence of the holy angels, and in the presence of the Lamb: ¹¹ And the smoke of their torment ascendeth up for ever and ever: and they have no rest day nor night, who worship the beast and his image, and whosoever receiveth the mark of his name. (Revelation 14:9-11)

If a person decides to take that 666 Mark (on their right hand or forehead – notice how specific prophecy can be?), then they doom themselves to eternity in the fires of Hell.

Don't take the Mark! Better still, take God's rescue plan to be supernaturally removed before the hellhole that Earth will become, and thereby avoid the 666 Mark altogether!

CONCLUSION: Now, the hope promised

These end-times prophecies are sure to come, make no mistake about it. It is genuine real, wrath-of-God stuff worse than your wildest nightmares. Yet, there is hope in that there is an escape clause, a rescue plan, for whosoever wants and will take it. It is called, The Rapture, a supernatural event in which people will be literally snatched off the Earth by Divine power to be brought to reside safely up in Heaven before all those terrors are loosed upon the world.

God loves you. He really does!

But, there is a problem. You and I have defied Him and broken His laws. This is called sin. The penalty is, I am afraid, very severe: death in Hell! He is so holy and pure, He cannot abide the presence of evil. But, because God loves us, He chose to make a way back to Him, a way to get reconciled. He sent Jesus to come to earth to be born as one of us, fully a man, and yet never losing His Divinity as the Son of God. He grew up, sharing in this life, but never committing any sin Himself. Then at the right time, He voluntarily stepped into our place to die the death our sins deserved. That was what He was doing on the cross, suffering, bleeding and dying for us so we wouldn't have to die.

Someone has said that Jesus got what He didn't deserve (death)

So that we could get what we don't deserve (life).

The final deal is this:
If we will place our faith, our trust, in Jesus, that:

1) He died for our sins
2) was buried
3) and rose from the dead three days later

then God says we will be accepted and forgiven.

If you are not sure you will escape the fire of Hell and instead make it to Heaven, then pray, and tell God in your own words that you are trusting in Jesus, like the three points above. Do that in honesty from the heart, and you will that very moment be forgiven, and going to heaven! Moreover, because of the Rapture, you will escape the coming night of the terrible Tribulation period's seven years.

Here is a sample prayer you can use if you want:
Lord, I know I have sinned. I know now that I deserve death. I thank You that Jesus died in my place to pay for my sins. I believe also that He was buried, and that He rose from the dead three days later. Thank You for the forgiveness of all my sins. I pray this in the name of Jesus Christ. Amen.

Afterword

The prophesied terrible future on Earth will not last forever. As said before, the 70th Week lasts seven years. At the end of those seven years, Jesus Christ will return to Earth in the Second Coming. Besides the terrifying judgments revealed, Revelation also prophesies about glories to come.

1 And I saw a new heaven and a new earth: for the first heaven and the first earth were passed away; and there was no more sea.
2 And I John saw the holy city, new Jerusalem, coming down from God out of heaven, prepared as a bride adorned for her husband.
3 And I heard a great voice out of heaven saying, Behold, the tabernacle of God is with men, and he will dwell with them, and they shall be his people, and God himself shall be with them, and be their God.
4 And God shall wipe away all tears from their eyes; and there shall be no more death, neither sorrow, nor crying, neither shall there be any more pain: for the former things are passed away.
5 And he that sat upon the throne said, Behold, I make all things new. And he said unto me, Write: for these words are true and faithful.
6 And he said unto me, It is done. I am Alpha and Omega, the beginning and the end. I will give unto him that is athirst of the fountain of the water of life freely.
7 He that overcometh shall inherit all things; and I will be his God, and he shall be my son. (Revelation 21:1-7)

The Apostle John wrote about the matter of that "overcometh":

4 For whatsoever is born of God overcometh the world: and this is the victory that overcometh the world, even our faith.
5 Who is he that overcometh the world, but he that believeth that Jesus is the Son of God? (1 John 5:4-5)

If you, reader, have placed your trust in Jesus Christ for the forgiveness of your sins, then John's words are talking about YOU as an overcomer.

When God refers to Himself as "the alpha and the omega", He is using the first and last letters in the Greek alphabet. Its meaning is that He is the eternal One who was there at the beginning and will be there forever, for there is no end to eternity.

The resurrection will fit every believer with a new, glorious, immortal body that will last for eternity, for our mortal bodies would not last that long.

Something some people don't understand about eternity is that it will be fun!

[11] Thou wilt shew me the path of life: in thy presence is fulness of joy; at thy right hand there are pleasures for evermore. (Psalm 16:11)

I hope to see you there!

If you have placed your faith in Jesus Christ, you will definitely be there!

Resources

1 https://believersportal.com/list-bible-prophecies/
2 https://www.biblestudytools.com/bible-study/topical-studies/the-old-testament-is-filled-with-fulfilled-prophecy-11652232.html
3 Ibid
4 Ibid
5 Ibid
6 Ibid
7 https://subspla.sh/7g9j9t6
8 Ibid
9 Ibid
10 Ibid
11 https://biblehub.com/commentaries/ezekiel/38-6.htm
12 https://hope4israel.org/jerusalem-70-ad-not-one-stone-left-upon-another/
13 https://www.azbible.com/prophecies-given-by-jesus.html
14 Ibid
15 Ibid
16 Ibid